Cheerleader's Guide to the World : Council Book

Cheerleader's Guide to the World : Council Book

Stacy Doris

Roof Books
New York

ISBN: 1-931824-18-5
Library of Congress Catalog Card Number: 2006921661

Cover art: "Venus Table" from The Grolier Codex (13th c. Mayan)
Originally published in *The Maya Scribe and His World*
by Michael Coe, 1973. (The Grolier Club, New York)

Author photo by Chet Wiener
Football plays by Bill Baker

to Rayzl

Roof Books are distributed by
Small Press Distribution
1341 Seventh Avenue
Berkeley, CA. 94710-1403.
Phone orders: 800-869-7553
www.spdbooks.org

State of the Arts
NYSCA

This book was made possible, in part, with public funds from the New York State Council on the Arts, a state agency.

Roof Books
are published by
Segue Foundation
303 East 8th Street
New York, NY 10009
segue.org

Cheerleader's Guide to the World : Council Book

Concentrating on my life's work about Money-Love-Writing (how they're the same fault) which involves Ancient Greek and Arabic metrics, I got to thinking of Pindar as a cheerleader so I started writing this which I thought would be part of that but it isn't really. Plus living here now in the West which means going to Central America to swim as often as possible, I started considering Mesoamerican time and its ballgames which bring me to our own.

N0t Righ+ N0w is based on the name of one of the grandfathers and fathers of the four great houses of the Lord Quichés in the Popol Vuh. I cast them as football triplets.

The leader is Laugh1ng M1rrors Puk1ng, short for Love Money Poetry.

I rearranged the word "culture" to "cultrue"
and "field", "filled", "filed" are interchangeable.
There are a few variations on "leadership" as well.

The team and its town are known roughly as Twisted or Deception High. So's everyplace here.

The text in general is a sort of sandwich-translation read-through of four books: *Popol Vuh*, *Paterson*, *Tibetan Book of the Dead*, and the *Secret Autobiographies of Jigme Lingpa*

Hi. I'm Tanesia
and a cheerleader
Exarchon stationed
right in the push. Since
for our language "bless"
comes from "bleeding"
subtlety's violence.
Because names get lost.

To win we gotta imitate
sameness. That's full time.

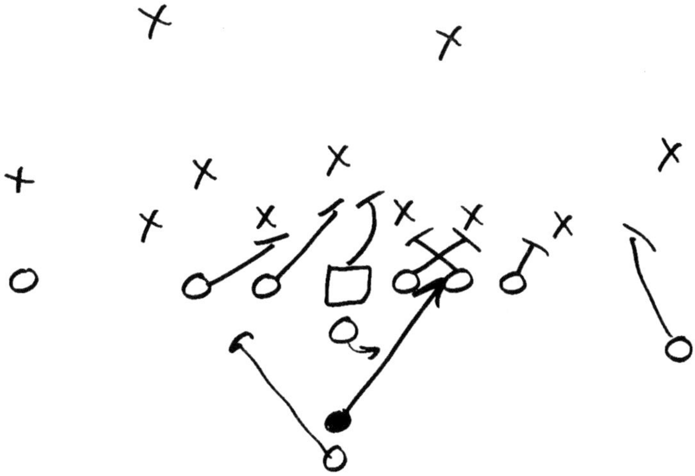

Here's what I wrote 30 years after
the meltdown: when I was -15:

The good old idea
was that corn growth
+ tax cuts make leisure.

Though agriculture means
"slash and burn" and "dispersed
population" maybe it wasn't
as bad as that sounds.

This is about Our Country and Our Cultrue
since even before they were Ours.

That's why it sandwiches Popol Vuh Paterson
Tibetan Dead Jigme Lingpa Pindar

Rah rah:

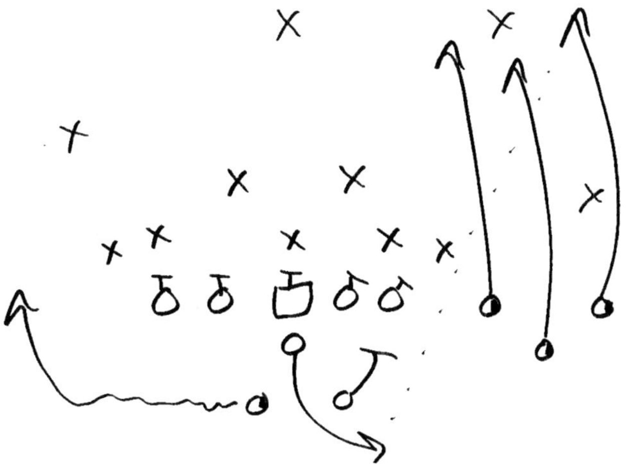

A green bird taught the kids art. But then
he got plugged by Laugh1ng M1rrors Puk1ing

who crams him good shoves him in bed
and goes off from shame leaving the desert
sphere's intricate cultrue of offense in the infant
stage hands of stage hands. Religion aims
to keep continuity going and clearly
say our 'leaders that makes war.

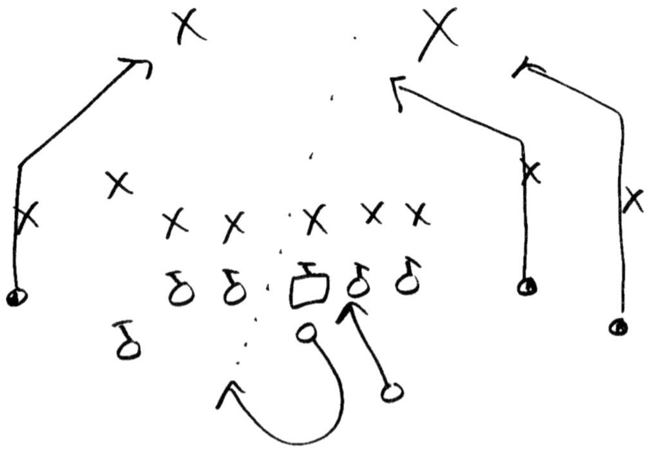

Out there on the field of Twisted
or Deception High with the sign
Puk1ing like an SUV commercial
on our display-energy screen
which is the same plasma
of the mall heap world
of undifferentiated empty
5ungla55e5 won out for good
as our coach. Then we
'leaders began avoiding
our impulses and memory
to burn out on practice
and team spirit bulimics

something to look
back on when we're old.

So growing corn showed
the preponderance of land and sky plus the need for oil
not mixing and that
'leads to what Laugh1ng M1rrors call genetic drift
or stealth or "multilogic" or "hidden
under green and blue
pompoms."

Or Bisquick: greased with the destructive Private
Properties of lubricants.

A Muffin Box recipe:

Force manifests in space thus counting the field it
inserts we're fucked yes this was a typical bakeoff.
Like each hour's measured but so are the minutes
with the same numbers: why?
The slots of time filled with M1rrors.

<<gloss has an extra-societal relationship with life>>>

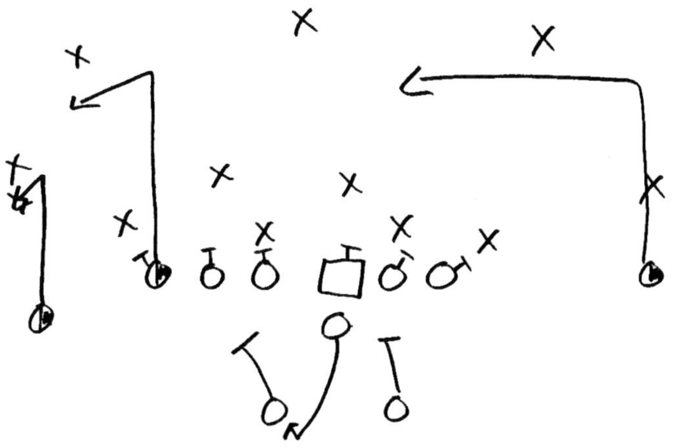

When I was a child
and it thundered I called
out to the corn not to be
frightened which helps but not
if Laugh1ng M1rrors tries it.
When the tv came to tell him
he'd been elected he was.

Came is death's name: came saw.
Bundles them up stash 'em
under the porch with their gullets
full of mush and hope

except there aren't any walls.
Only they don't die we just
disappear them by forgetting
and otherwise. Who because
they don't know their sources
train their bodies to aim
armored not ideas.

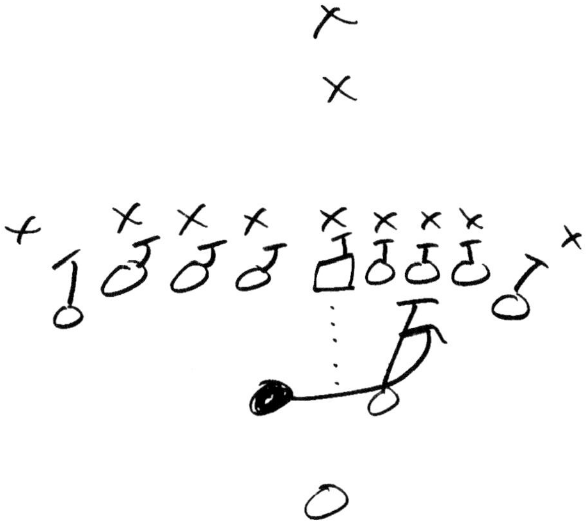

Let them snake lolling
under and quick to strike
reconciled: the people and the cars.

Has its own players but they're
composite due to what keeps
forgotten as if improvised
makeshift like artistry and that
were unending. So even if the filed
has a story: it's infinite a language
of freedom in drivel or as
Laugh1ng M1rrors cries: invent.

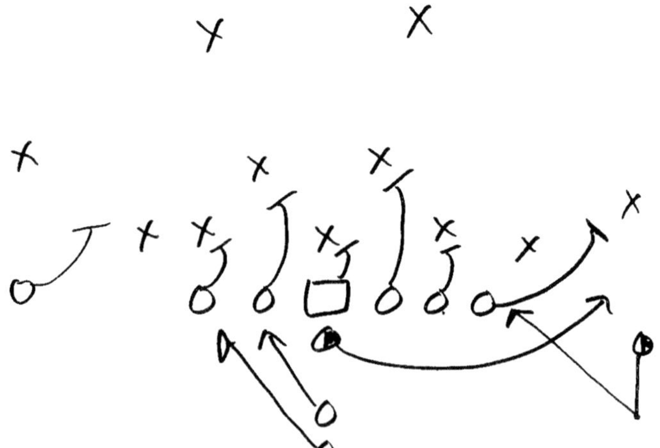

We cheerleaders are a bra
for the team: support support
as if girls
could be citizens
we mouth the tunes
of bellicose stasis
because time only seems
to advance and we won't

let it.
We're puppets since words
sing through us from wherever not
ours into everyone we're screwed

or on a pulse give me
an A

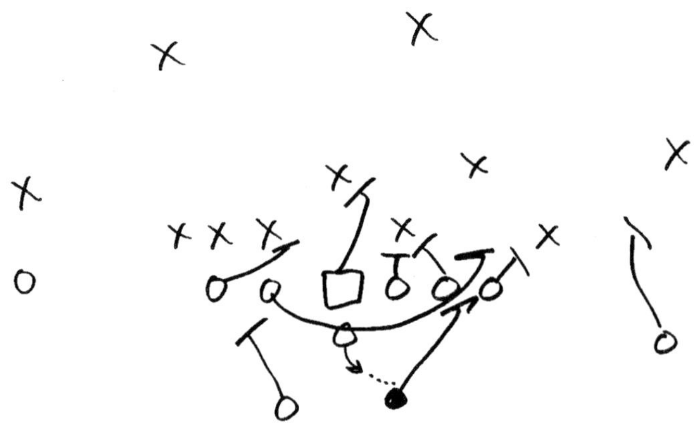

Figures explain lives
that's why cheering counts.
Democracy's based on
numbers so invisible
the sky ever clean

in Democracy time isn't
there but the filed synchronizes
bodies and pools them
humming in blood into one
model alone.

Make in the game is stint
what vanishes a reaped
answer to meaning with bare hands.
Dare by multiplying that skips all steps.
Or how locate sense
when it's camped in belief?
By sniffle? By defect?
By addition? Binge?
Tackling trees? The corn:
knowledge resolute in
stupidness well packed.

Soured rows heavy
In the slot of a halftime.

What's human is formations
and drills. In the mix not the
matter or match. The commercial
habitat ploughed tracked stolen
or too glorified and thought
may be boating.

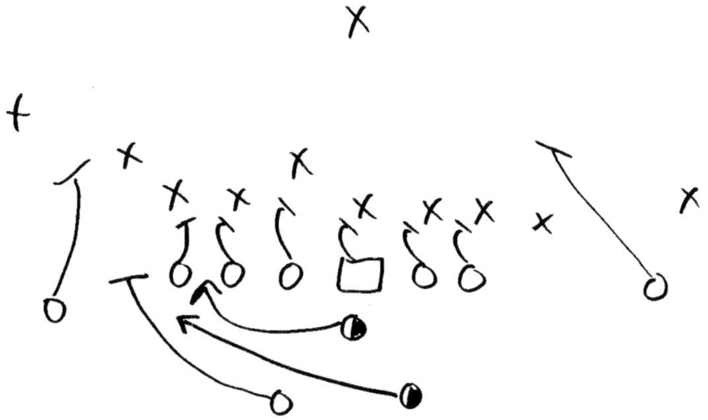

The town's name is Twisted
Or Deceptive just out there.
Nobody N0t Righ+ N0w ever
purchased it but stunted
the lakes into this. When we fall
or press our ears to the ground
or jump high we cheerleaders
hear water. Or anyone sleeping
does. The ravished eddies say.
Or minnows. So we breathe in corn
our consistency. Not even accident
marks the blank lawns and conical
trees the gleaming driveways
jungle gyms.

So the one I kissed magnified
himself in Laugh1ng M1rrors
Puk1ing his name like a sign
claims he's our day
because his eyes are mental
only it's not true. His face can't
touch everywhere just
the ground beneath us
was a nuance always choked.

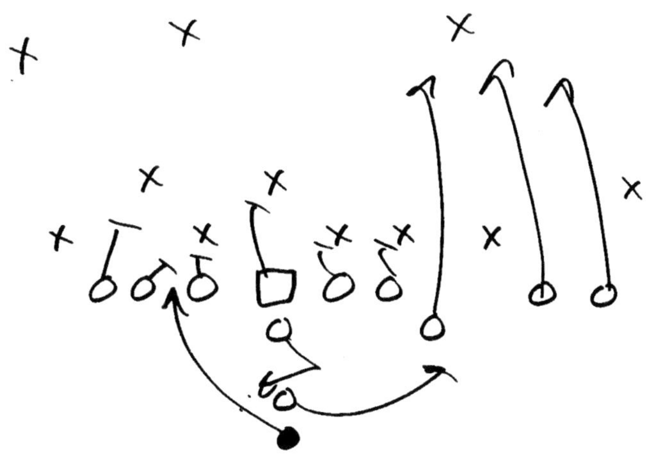

No one could outhrow
N0t Righ+ N0w so when
they play nothing
happens. Thunderstorms.

If you close your eyes
and they're out there
you hear static the
drone in a seashell wafted
toward bleachers almost
a confession how the sides
drag each other into motion
and physics just orbits
like wicks demand in gutters
in flame. Be avid be vigilant

it goads. A conversation. It
needs to be heard this way.
Listening with your eyes
closed you realize how the ball
actually moves in a spiral:
Susurrus. A fat chance.

Drink to them for me
I'm too young. Stalks and birds
looked on their practice.

This is the team what N0t
Righ+ N0w call them: there's
Scab Stripper and Blood Hoard
they save up. There's Pus
Mound and Ear Lob they make
the others redden. There's Cheek
and Bone Meat who grind. Then
Socks and Shorts bring woe upon
the messy which is all teenagers.

Wracked as surfers on
real waves these thoughts
so their bodies in slicing's
crests interlace repel
and pivot land a whirlpool of leaf
and curds forgetfulness
regroup coalesce at the rim
molten they plunge
to all conclusions as if
atomic bobbing ribbons
drunken feathers whole

unsupported catastrophies
hitting the agility exhausted
so fury only's left offense
gravity so rebound cupped
and predictable a loss
still courses still upriver

filled air with spume
as if its equals. A charge
spins in their arteries call

though no words
remain so the storms
in their own minds elude
them and they falter
but receive but gain
yards. The field's

a shore of missing
reservoirs packed crystalline the bleachers

so N0t Righ+ N0w weren't
on the Team and the Team
wanted them. "Come practice with us
here in Twisted or Deceit

mark lost oaks ankles."

So N0t Righ+ N0w just
slid down over an edge
to a mouth where the canyons
leafhopper tick stink bug
and came to a fork where
they lost the pass
noticing their opponents
are fake.

Their opponents are scarecrows
or effigies but that's beside the point.
It was fumble one time out
and the bench of coals
not real either but
singed our boys
good and the Team laughed.
The Team said they'd
get them tomorrow quick.
The Team's ball is just
an ovoid knife.

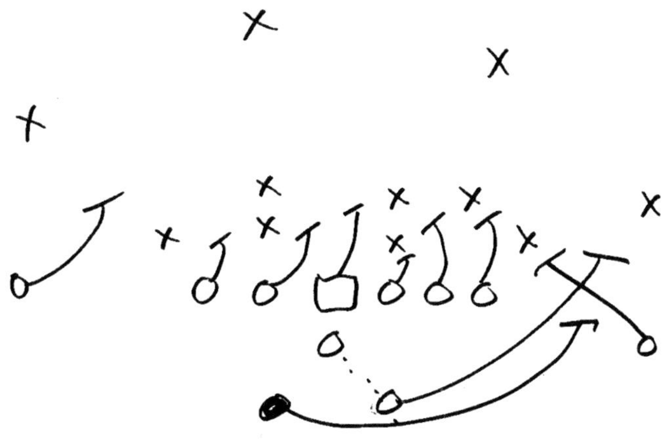

Everything's a big lie
except maybe its qualities
that nobody can recognize
because we see in globs.
Cheer leaders visualize in quantity alone.
Understand this N0t Righ+
N0w. Once there's no winning
you can score.

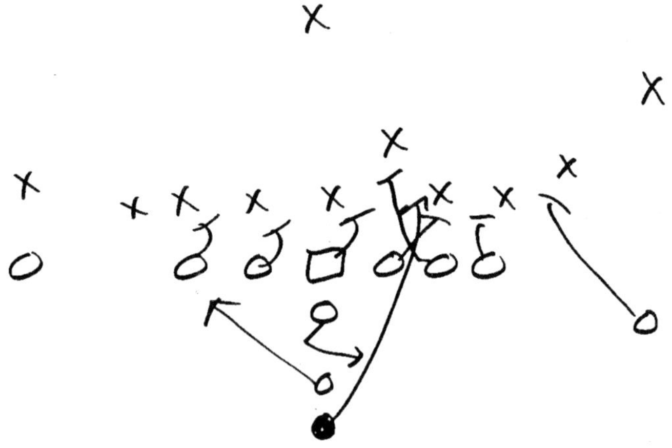

In a huddle's drunken push
in a tent with no matches
rattle gnashed jaws
choke then bats razor
next Laugh1ng M1rror wants
the candle back they'd
borrowed but it's gone
so we're in debt and
that's government or
'leadership: our heads
turning to pumpkins

a touch down. Dark then:

Girls bound by an instinct
to act the same like ribbons
drawn to the team
indiscriminately fucked
drawn to a bulge
a fork in the corn a bone
saying you don't want
yes I do say the girls two
disappeared for good
she stretched out her
hand and they took
it spitting
this was the word Twister
girls disparate
in pouring.

N0t Righ+ N0w
a mash of detail relying
on the filed huddled to curl
like a newborn
if there's summer or a breeze
one corn ear
branch enough giraffish
so an axis.
Only the shortest life is fearless.

By the stalks briefly enlivened
unafraid they huddle which
is to say burn within flowering

still as history so fanged
into crops. Bleachers mount
our only growth the ruckus
of bones tinny mixed.

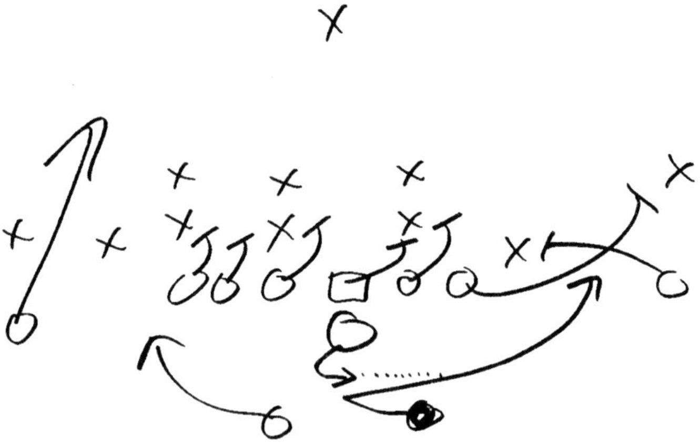

Laugh1ng M1rrors Puk1ing
in whose chinks we conspire
on oxygen and plot and wish for bed
and huddle just a little more
sentient pre-clobbered
perhaps already gone
live this midget circle

parallel yet slashing
cross-current on the filled
charged last down hollows
assisted as if rumored worlds
could be of a instinct
less foundational

or so rippling as thoughts
might empty upstream
in the field crouched
unlike as snowflakes
eccentric still encoded
by vengeance and its ilk
patient but not nearly
enough landlocked vitriol
combed strategies in muck
in limp stalks no sleep.

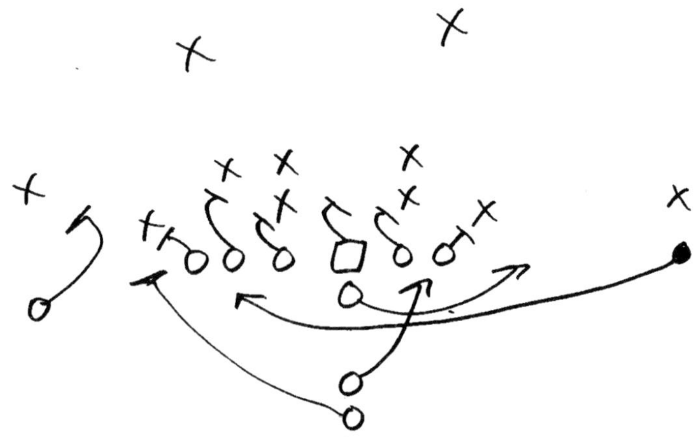

You lazy idiots
why give your all
instead of just exactly
what it takes too idle
to calculate only
one speed full ahead
wasting you think
because there are
daisies you will flourish
because snow melts
we'll infiltrate

Hey: whatever others' ideas
are are just dust
in a vacuum while we know
how to charge
and be our own surfaces
only: past defeat yeah.
Something else the same.

Or 'leadershop begets
empire leading to
insubordination: calling for respect
their mouths jiggle
in this damp
known as sunshine.
That's the secret of guzzle

gas runny noses
unmentionable fouls blunt
diversions that clamber up
snake and wet concealed
in the huddle a flickering
a tremble somehow.

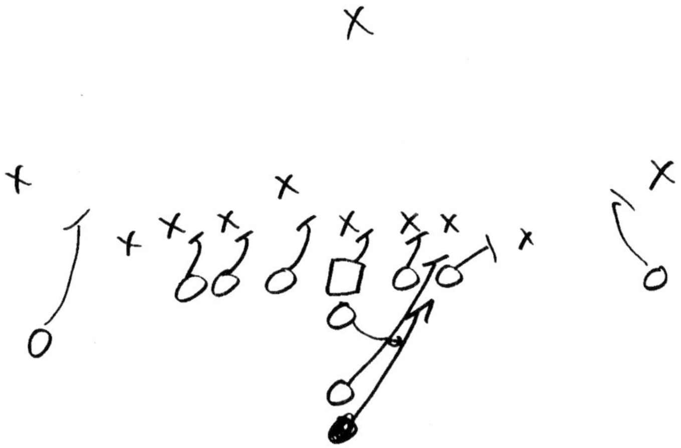

Outside there's a world
subject to my incursions
rubble a playground female
for concrete
action and resources
so what if it fights back
cliffside in proof
numbering as proof
skid along proof
outpaced their dogs

Wait! Those ugly young
legs rough worked arms
to toss
Yah Yah Yah Yah Yah
back now down girl

breathless surveys after
(ours but expensive)
possessively tilted weight
on the ball other thigh
lift arm swing forward

clever if we're monkeys.

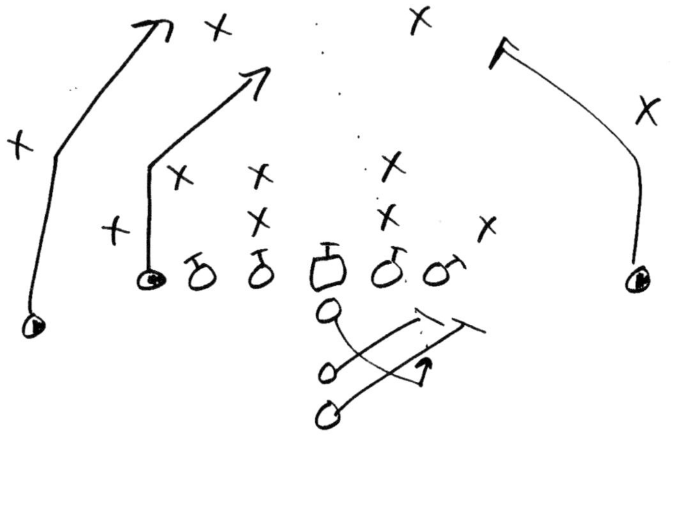

Clever if we were monkeys.

Even our mother laughs so
to see us we can never
go home. Consigned to
trees and field howling
in zigzags pestered by birds.

Or not a court just used furrows
razors of grass taunted by
grasshoppers like icons. Monkeys

because no change means no win
and sacrifice the only perpetual
agility itself honed. Plus victory

takes brains but not for thinking.
Let go to grab
the next branch trades
from limb to limb to limb.

So N0t Righ+ N0w pottered
jog from nowhere with the ball
whooping as defense arms
behind like mockery
the sudden birth of loudmouths.

Every morning with lunchboxes
they set off to school but never
got there caught in outwitting
termites until that lead them
to the filed. They found a ball

learned to throw
without first catching. So
aim was random and their minds
siphoned. The proxy
face of Laugh1ng M1rrors
loomed up as usual on every
screen to bait classrooms
in the name of safety. All learning's
uniform and so they had straight As.

Where is what's ours? Come on
and name it. That's my cheer

sorta. What's true is all
that can't be formulated and this
is how N0t Righ+ N0w learned.
So went to meet the Team down
non-existent hills and such
to Twisted or Deception. It wasn't
their idea just inertia just where
we all end up: some kind of camp.

Walking ‘cuz there’s no pavement
for skateboards among stalks
brought two fleas and a mosquito
as their mascots. The red path choked
lots barren with chipmunks
just pocketing flint along chronic
swooped dens of four-leaf clover plenty
gerbil picnics hoop recreation
other marks of appeasement
so slavery inaudible commanding
since all words

rouse more or less.
And the thunder voice Laugh1ng
on everyday blood shuck
lips blowing after hikers.

Making equal's the same as
digesting for amoebas to delegate
materials in rank and shape
via mechanics. A Team channels
kids into sequences since bodies
unaltered mean bombardment.
Commodities depend on equivalence
in all of us so I nod

hi to the Team someone
a liar spoke unnoticed. "This
is no guys just scarecrows."
Hey Pus Mound and Ear Lob
Scab Stripper Hoard Cheek Meat
Socks and Short with their motto
Cell Death: "What's
happening? They've gone
and hurt our feelings now we're
sore." "Let's play" said N0t
Righ+ N0w and were asked "Where
you come from?" "Over the hill"
and there were no hills so "we
don't know. Let's play." "Okay
here's our ball" "No our ball
first" "No ours" and on. A
draw. That night

they slept in a pitchfork's dark
and finches which the Team
intended to clear them out
for good but they were already

preempted so it didn't make
a dent. For N0t Righ+ N0w awareness
was an optical illusion. Still
all toads are proof of Laugh1ng
M1rrors. "Let's search for it"
they dumbly agreed. The prints
can be a curled and small
as pubic hairs and clear
as if etched in mud. That
determined them. Once again
broke through dissolved windows
like the tubes
spitting in old tvs.

The team charts the field
in chalk pictures of moves
conducting to amounts of eternities:
a waste. Any place is not separating
imputations each spot's the vase
of Forever Young our State
where display equals juice
spread into those dense
populations we call outer.
The good vessel Blowjob
innumerably pigeonholed
lapis in the sky not outshone
for that: N0t Righ+ N0w couldn't
help but reach briefly. Hot potato.

Comparing for the future
enthralled set down in code then

the basic inner filed
has six qualities beyond scuffmarks
churning out display
energy via random
obedience and discipline.

Who could explain anyhow
to the crowd of no experience
other than roughly
"it's like that" where representing
goes poof. For younger kids run
make legends out of actions
and squeal at the trace of some
ghost or mishap. The glory
of conceitedness.

So at daybreak with the mascots
still sleeping N0t Righ+ N0w spaced
out into upwards pure howling
animal brace cluster
density as in a lapse
of recalling and saw
red with a little blue mixed in.

The team aimed to beat them
preemptively from above.
But N0t Righ+ N0w
make deals with: fire bats chewing gum.
They sleep on their stakeboards
in their Gameboys and beebees.

Except something (a spook?) grabbed
N0t's head from the barrel and tossed it.
So Righ+ N0w tacked a cabbage
and that worked. They play
without their brains in any case.
Their thoughts are the ordinary sky
including hurricanes.

Relying on death as what
can be trusted. N0t Righ+ N0w
came to their so-called
end. Here it is: the epitaph.
The team showed the way
so they climbed right in the
flood. Pus Mound said
it was a test to jump
over and heroes prefer
to fail that sort of laden
thing so they got in
and merrily sank. Their bones
sang Cucaracha.

"Wouldn't
it be fun to dump their bones
in the canyon?" But of course
there's no canyon. The team
poured them in the sewer.

The moon was going down.
A sound said "this is hell."
But the triplets know hell's
a product of thoughts and
they don't use theirs minds
so what's the big deal?

Other than fully perfecting
the display energy harnessed
from air a condensation
of all refugees there's no
other way to run out.

Then there's no difference
between fans and sports
N0t Righ+ N0w realized and since
they're flooded by savings
and commercial breaks words
in thought bubbles
gurgled from all Laugh1ng
M1rrors Puk1ng. At one point
they burst like vultures etc.
to what would be Twisted
or Decieve a valley
crammed in stalks. A crowd
roared and they said "try
this" and crashed. Pray:

Violence is everything
the cultrue can discern.

In the year of Gila Monsters Stewed
in Cloths of Excrements on the tenth
day of Muck they remembered
their father then promptly forgot.

And so N0t Righ+ N0w reappeared
from death. Spectators saw them
on the water scruffy and flat.
Amen they shouted from behind
the bleachers. And half time got
underway.

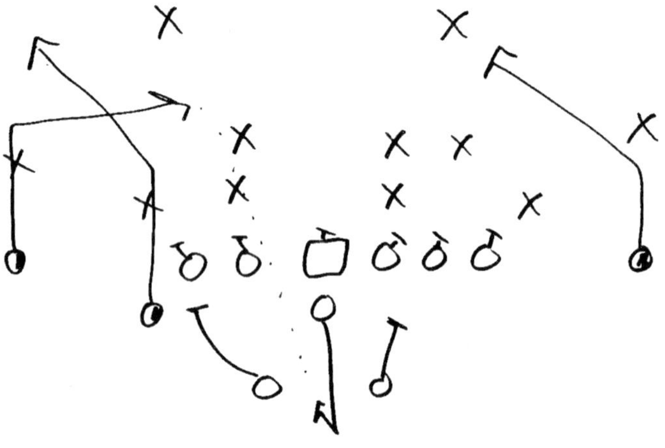

Defeat is just a kind
of reawakening inhabited
by throngs as if cities
existed. So disguised for Halloween
as dumb bumblebees N0t
Righ+ N0w started tricking.

Set bunnies and themselves
allegedly on fire and the Team
saw and cried
do it to us so they did
and burned them bad
because grace is a byproduct
of sacrifice in the cultrue
just like plenty of exercise.

"Bumblebees immolate yourselves"

cried the Team so we took
Righ+'s legs and arms spread
'em wide and cracked
the head rolled straight off
again heart dug swaddled
on a stick and the crowd went
wild calling "now get up"
Righ+ did while the Team
clamored "do it to us" so they got
burned. They'd asked for it.
Every high school understands going amuck.

Hey Team! Now you've arrived
at so-called death. Dig in and relish it.

But was it N0t Righ+ N0w
or just impersonations some kind
of hostage crisis? Concurrently
they shoot pool. These
are examples of relationships
between joint effort and the
natural environment. Not
static values. The skunk
can substitute for the willow-
fart whenever. Anyhow we
were not being funny just weird.

So if N0t Righ+ N0w defeated
the team it was by mere
transformation. And then they called
themselves. They said their names.

Meanwhile we had a bake sale.

We frosted the cakes and called
them for our piercings: Middle
of My Nipple Middle of My Eyebrow
Middle of My Septum Middle of
My Cunt Lip Middle of the Night.
All for the cause of team effort.

A girlfriend could be pieced
together from these scraps
but they forgot the vital
organs so it couldn't really last.

They tried to fuck us and we
tried to fuck them too but some
of our insides kept missing. Hey

yeah the ultimate orgasm's
voidness' peak and yeah we had
our labia but more vital parts
were needed in between etc.
I'm telling you. We're made
pretty much of cornflakes.

Like the first time they tried
to make us out of binge
and barf only and our socialization
was perfect unbound by
body parts we didn't need
to move an inch for anything
we appeared unrivaled

which is really not attractive
so they marred our understanding.
The root was implanted.

Then our own cheering faces
in the M1rror of the filled
were what we didn't recognize
surrounded by banners
umbrellas big blow pops and so on
with giant rainbow balloons
and display screens all over

in cubicles and drive-throughs
in the leaking tents of Forever
Young. In the plains wind.

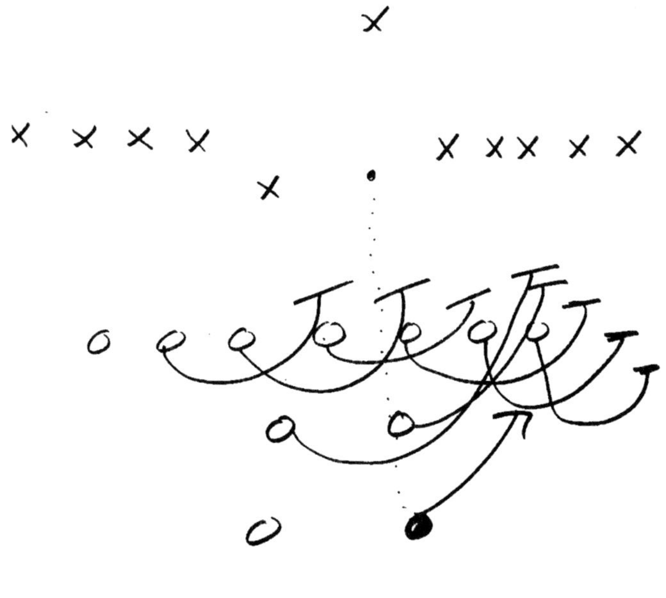

the opposite
of minusing thoughts
Righ+ sort of dozed
in a blood loan shackled
and battering though limp
to balance while there's
none in our cultrue only
weight. Unconscious Righ+
looked for the rebus
of addition a sense beyond
what counts. Dazzled which we
always seem so never
victorious or radiant. Laugh1ng
M1rrors Puk1ng legislates
zones from slaughter called
exercise and building
physiques dental hygiene. In an
odd updraft views down
looking scathed.

Evolution lost its pull
over Righ+ in the new
impure magic face state.
Because his body
got intuitive and mental
nothing really could hurt him
which is just a perception.
Why do anything else?

Except only sacrifice
conducts our progress.
So N0t Righ+ N0w ripped
themselves open: arms
sides lobes. Cut themselves
saying "We don't belong
here." So they packed
a lunch and went camping.
Kept together pressed on.

Fire burns
and the flames
spread everywhere
once talk fans
them. M1rrors
Laugh1ng Puk1ng
maneuvers it so
to write or buy or
love is a fire which
is not much being
in a position to write
or buy or love
but the big trick's
also an attack and
there appears
no way to stop it
when anyone
gets going.

It isn't very clear
how they made it
past oceans. Crossed
as if there were
no water in
the first place.

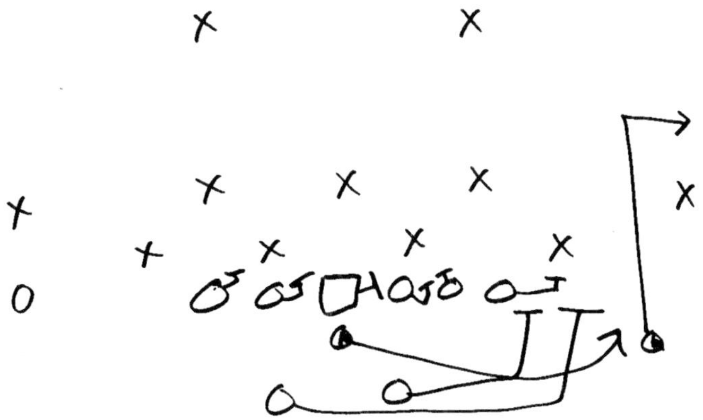

To be proud of Laugh1ng
M1rrors Puk1ng of ourselves
for team spirit blindness
definitely helps. N0t
Righ+ N0w huddle their eyes
bulging from the smoke
pit old guys from there
light up cigars imitate
torture or torture. Inhale
okay they say Okay? Okay!
and the flames swoop
over whatever was drunk
in the image of M1rrors Puk1ng
up love trade.

Molten so praised bottle
bent to sand congratulations.
An improved carnage.

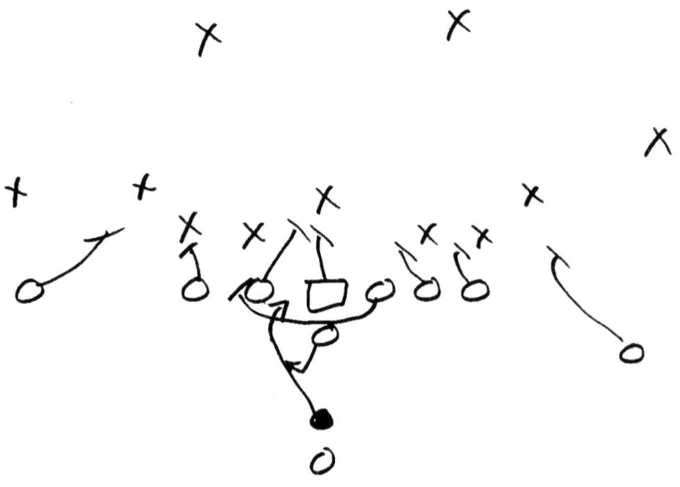

Just think behind a wrapped
verandah porch
upstairs some room
with a cheerleader's throbbing
slim best-proportioned filed
ornaments relaxed and spontaneous:
who will win this shot
for himself?
        She's so easy
wanting to chant the same
words over
hold sight and breath
prisoners in the one place
a pond of no separations.

If you're serious: milk her.
Using passion on impulse
instrumentalizes movements.

Yeah! Lose to win!
Scatter yourselves!
Bloodspill depicts
the reason for life.
Rain's made of it.
Go quench your thirst.

N0t Righ+ N0w would lie
by the river soaking rays.
The team SMSed us
“work out shoreside”
they said “naked doing
your downward dog stuff
let them fuck you until
you figure out.” This before
we quit answering
so had to. But our asses

weren't shiny enough
they didn't want us
instead we got all
bit up from wasps
our tits and
butts welted and the team
was so mad they didn't
speak to us for weeks
hoping it was all our

fault getting scared
shitless by the triplets'
libdoless or homo habits.

The filed's a door
to any other real estate
maybe the ball is too.
So Laugh1ng M1rrors
Puk1ing recast the whole mall
converted to an instrument
bent on his agenda
more than boasting.
Then his friends all

had it good at the expense
of the world. Each of them
counted as triplets guzzle
genomes. At the checkout
of No Busses Go There.
At the Imax like any great
score. And N0t Righ+ N0w
opened their very own
kiosk.

I cheered it on.

Bulldozed through the filled's
whole stratosphere barrage
to make a border fire to
link so as imprison until memorials
alone are respite so howl

takeover as whirling the flame
confused by stuff once
nameless with a yippee
who can afford that? Upwind

to smithereens
all of Deception or Twisted
like a skirt on a grate bloats
and exposes fizzle unparalleled
let Laugh1ng M1irros explain
and we'll be the updraft
its heart this surface glimmer

dig in and you get zero.
Relying on a .jpg
glossy booming hurrah
white-hot girls us
craters what we're made of
mud in the current is
that losing? Broke our
jaws and so we cheered:
blazing stealth tops genius
N0t Righ+ N0w indistinguishable

from pools of blood
seeped us and on.

Laugh1ng M1rrors
Puk1ing's Grand Secret-talk:
Expression of My Realizations
40. In accordance with
all that's been said my plan
for the fusing of lucres
protected over lifetimes
matured like a Mother-Father
wave of industriousness
everywhere nosy as enlightened
surveillance. As a result
I forgot about grasping
and began to let my powers
aimlessly accrue like the whole
species they may well represent.

I bore in mind the substitutability
of one and all and spaced out
into the fact that life's my own
figment a.k.a suckling ragweed.

Thus I was sure that bucks
could be transmissible. This kept
me going forever. 42. A few days
later I thought "we the people
of this half-witted Greatland
where teaching is greed
and survival bellicosity we drift
orphaned of screen display-
energy and when is Oscar night
ever?" And I dozed off and
dreamed a big "symbol's
dissolved" which as it swept
into nonactuality I spilled
a great monument mall
in every vehicle's wake.

A sort of tailgate. Then I put
off reading the rest since
who made this appointment
for me after all? Who turned on
this channel? Anyhow
there was no way to study it
in order. I stashed a few
Master cards in my mouth
and headed home. On my way
I met Key Document The Ole'
Treasure Chest and remembered
the SLA robberies with Patti
Hearst in the role of my mother
and just as I thought it
she turned out to really
be my mother and code breaker
saying "you should keep
all this more secret. That this
is the instrument of all
liberation's beside the point.
So you went and ate it."

Therefore she made me
gobble down the rest
and the figures and measures
got stamped on my insides
what can I do? I have no

use for memory now. Our
National Credit Line
remains unrivaled in the Pure
Vision Family Mode despite
such claims being common
these days which makes
consumers doubt but then
do palms still have hands

anymore? And I cried myself
to sleep remembering when
to identify scattered perceptions
through the public display-
energy of just a few MHZ
and elements was "art"
before the wave. Still

if a summons comes even
now you'll go to jury duty
right? I made the big
decision to relax and set
it aside for years. But signs
are all anyone believes in
so I met thrice Dry-Me Out
who convinced me to scatter
the code in writing on surfaces
of paper. The thing is

like a gob of sesame seeds
in puff pastry Dry-Me Out's
subjugation's so uniformly
handsome and swoony to
my bubble-eye perspective
I'm finally blessed.
His cock's
the length of all moonlight
and just as unfailing
creeps upon one. Our worldy

aspirations then nigh
we nationally enact
slow as possible so fast
in repeated sequential demands.
46. But still from that same
story due to botching most

tender connections and with
emanated translators and
other precious writers

a variety of contradictions
flourish in particular friends
of the class effortlessly tricking.
They specialize in betrayal
of kindness ++. I managed through
effort to emulate them
but the impecunious won't
understand this and should
clever if we were monkeys.

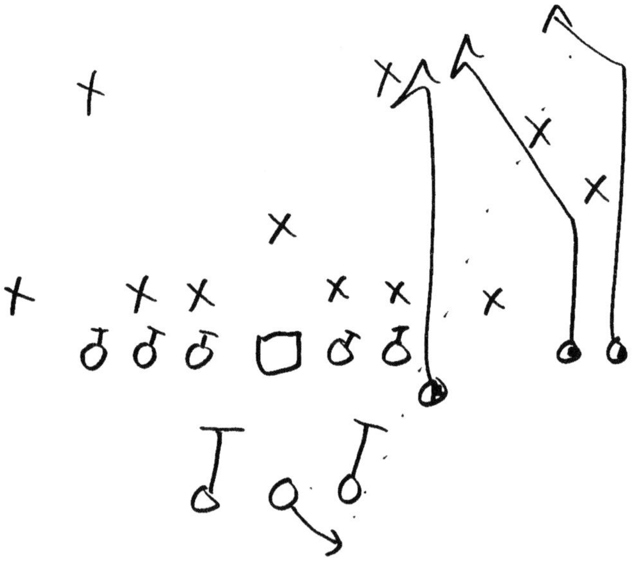

PS This is enough about N0t Righ+ N0w and the rest
given that there is no longer any place to see it. There is no more original recording now but even so everything has been completed here concerning it
which is now named High Stick.

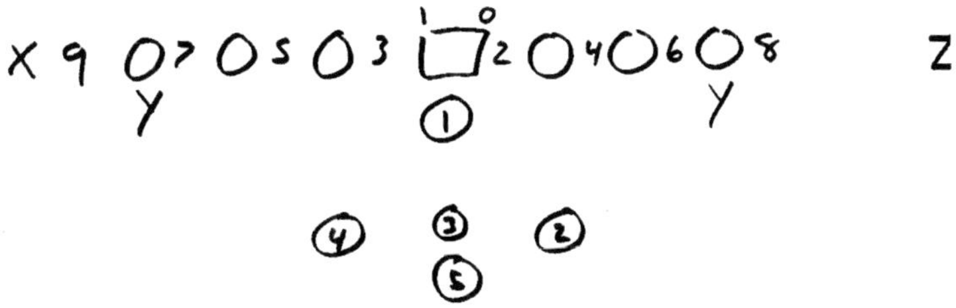

ROOF BOOKS

- ❑ Andrews, Bruce. **EX WHY ZEE**. 112p. $10.95.
- ❑ Andrews, Bruce. **Getting Ready To Have Been Frightened**. 116p. $7.50.
- ❑ Benson, Steve. **Blue Book**. Copub. with The Figures. 250p. $12.50
- ❑ Bernstein, Charles. **Controlling Interests**. 80p. $11.95.
- ❑ Bernstein, Charles. **Islets/Irritations**. 112p. $9.95.
- ❑ Bernstein, Charles (editor). **The Politics of Poetic Form**. 246p. $12.95; cloth $21.95.
- ❑ Brossard, Nicole. **Picture Theory**. 188p. $11.95.
- ❑ Cadiot, Olivier. **Former, Future, Fugitive**. Translated by Cole Swensen. 166p. $13.95.
- ❑ Champion, Miles. **Three Bell Zero**. 72p. $10.95.
- ❑ Child, Abigail. **Scatter Matrix**. 79p. $9.95.
- ❑ Davies, Alan. **Active 24 Hours**. 100p. $5.
- ❑ Davies, Alan. **Signage**. 184p. $11.
- ❑ Davies, Alan. **Rave**. 64p. $7.95.
- ❑ Day, Jean. **A Young Recruit**. 58p. $6.
- ❑ Di Palma, Ray. **Motion of the Cypher**. 112p. $10.95.
- ❑ Di Palma, Ray. **Raik**. 100p. $9.95.
- ❑ Doris, Stacy. **Kildare**. 104p. $9.95.
- ❑ Dreyer, Lynne. **The White Museum**. 80p. $6.
- ❑ Dworkin, Craig. **Strand**. 112p. $12.95.
- ❑ Edwards, Ken. **Good Science**. 80p. $9.95.
- ❑ Eigner, Larry. **Areas Lights Heights**. 182p. $12, $22 (cloth).
- ❑ Gardner, Drew. **Petroleum Hat**. 96p. $12.95.
- ❑ Gizzi, Michael. **Continental Harmonies**. 96p. $8.95.
- ❑ Gladman, Renee. **A Picture-Feeling**. 72p. $10.95.
- ❑ Goldman, Judith. **Vocoder**. 96p. $11.95.
- ❑ Gottlieb, Michael. **Ninety-Six Tears**. 88p. $5.
- ❑ Gottlieb, Michael. **Gorgeous Plunge**. 96p. $11.95.
- ❑ Gottlieb, Michael. **Lost & Found**. 80p. $11.95.
- ❑ Greenwald, Ted. **Jumping the Line**. 120p. $12.95.
- ❑ Grenier, Robert. **A Day at the Beach**. 80p. $6.
- ❑ Grosman, Ernesto. **The XULReader: An Anthology of Argentine Poetry (1981–1996)**. 167p. $14.95.
- ❑ Guest, Barbara. **Dürer in the Window, Reflexions on Art**.

Book design by Richard Tuttle. Four color throughout. 80p. $24.95.

- ❑ Hills, Henry. **Making Money**. 72p. $7.50. VHS videotape $24.95.
  Book & tape $29.95.
- ❑ Huang Yunte. **SHI: A Radical Reading of Chinese Poetry**. 76p. $9.95
- ❑ Hunt, Erica. **Local History**. 80 p. $9.95.
- ❑ Kuszai, Joel (editor) **poetics@**, 192 p. $13.95.
- ❑ Inman, P. **Criss Cross**. 64 p. $7.95.
- ❑ Inman, P. **Red Shift**. 64p. $6.
- ❑ Lazer, Hank. **Doublespace**. 192 p. $12.
- ❑ Levy, Andrew. **Paper Head Last Lyrics**. 112 p. $11.95.
- ❑ Mac Low, Jackson. **Representative Works: 1938–1985**.
  360p. $18.95 (cloth).
- ❑ Mac Low, Jackson. **Twenties**. 112p. $8.95.
- ❑ McMorris, Mark. **The Café at Light**. 112p. $12.95.
- ❑ Moriarty, Laura. **Rondeaux**. 107p. $8.
- ❑ Neilson, Melanie. **Civil Noir**. 96p. $8.95.
- ❑ Osman, Jena. **An Essay in Asterisks**. 112p. $12.95.
- ❑ Pearson, Ted. **Planetary Gear**. 72p. $8.95.
- ❑ Perelman, Bob. **Virtual Reality**. 80p. $9.95.
- ❑ Perelman, Bob. **The Future of Memory**. 120p. $14.95.
- ❑ Piombino, Nick, **The Boundary of Blur**. 128p. $13.95.
- ❑ Prize Budget for Boys, **The Spectacular Vernacular Revuew**. 96p. $14.95.
- ❑ Raworth, Tom. **Clean & Will-Lit**. 106p. $10.95.
- ❑ Robinson, Kit. **Balance Sheet**. 112p. $11.95.
- ❑ Robinson, Kit. **Democracy Boulevard**. 104p. $9.95.
- ❑ Robinson, Kit. **Ice Cubes**. 96p. $6.
- ❑ Scalapino, Leslie. **Objects in the Terrifying Tense
  Longing from Taking Place**. 88p. $9.95.
- ❑ Seaton, Peter. **The Son Master**. 64p. $5.
- ❑ Sherry, James. **Popular Fiction**. 84p. $6.
- ❑ Silliman, Ron. **The New Sentence**. 200p. $10.
- ❑ Silliman, Ron. **N/O**. 112p. $10.95.
- ❑ Smith, Rod. **Music or Honesty**. 96p. $12.95
- ❑ Smith, Rod. **Protective Immediacy**. 96p. $9.95
- ❑ Stefans, Brian Kim. **Free Space Comix**. 96p. $9.95
- ❑ Tarkos, Christophe. **Ma Langue est Poétique—Selected Works**. 96p. $12.95.
- ❑ Templeton, Fiona. **Cells of Release**. 128p. with photographs. $13.95.
- ❑ Templeton, Fiona. **YOU—The City**. 150p. $11.95.
- ❑ Torres, Edwin. **The All-Union Day of the Shock Worker**. 112 p. $10.95.
- ❑ Tysh, Chris. **Cleavage**. 96p. $11.95.

- ❑ Ward, Diane. **Human Ceiling**. 80p. $8.95.
- ❑ Ward, Diane. **Relation**. 64p. $7.50.
- ❑ Watson, Craig. **Free Will**. 80p. $9.95.
- ❑ Watten, Barrett. **Progress**. 122p. $7.50.
- ❑ Weiner, Hannah. **We Speak Silent**. 76 p. $9.95
- ❑ Weiner, Hannah. **Page**. 136 p. $12.95
- ❑ Wellman, Mac. **Miniature**. 112 p. $12.95
- ❑ Wellman, Mac. **Strange Elegies**. 96 p. $12.95
- ❑ Wolsak, Lissa. **Pen Chants**. 80p. $9.95.
- ❑ Yasusada, Araki. **Doubled Flowering: From the Notebooks of Araki Yasusada**. 272p. $14.95.

ROOF BOOKS
are published by
Segue Foundation
300 Bowery
New York, NY 10012
Visit our website at **segue.org**

ROOF BOOKS are distributed by
SMALL PRESS DISTRIBUTION
1341 Seventh Avenue
Berkeley, CA. 94710-1403.
Phone orders: 800-869-7553
spdbooks.org